THE
COWHERD'S
SON

THE
COWHERD'S
SON

Rajiv Mohabir

 TUPELO PRESS
NORTH ADAMS, MASSACHUSETTS

The Cowherd's Son.
Copyright © 2017 Rajiv Mohabir. All rights reserved.

Library of Congress Cataloging-in-Publication Data

Names: Mohabir, Rajiv, author.
Title: The cowherd's son / Rajiv Mohabir.
Description: North Adams, Massachusetts : Tupelo Press, [2017] |
The Kundiman Poetry Prize. | Includes bibliographical references.
Identifiers: LCCN 2017000643 | ISBN 9781936797967 (pbk.
original : alk. paper)
Classification: LCC PS3613.O376 A6 2017 | DDC 811/.6—dc23

Cover and text designed and composed in Adobe Garamond and
Bank Gothic by Dede Cummings.
Cover art: "Dancing Demon" (2010) by Amalesh Das. Mixed
medium on canvas, 40 by 40 inches. Used with permission
of the artist (http://amaleshdas.com).

First paperback edition: May 2017.

Tupelo Press
P.O. Box 1767, North Adams, Massachusetts 01247
(413) 664–9611 / editor@tupelopress.org / www.tupelopress.org

Tupelo Press is an award-winning independent literary press that
publishes fine fiction, nonfiction, and poetry in books that are a
joy to hold as well as read. Tupelo Press is a registered 501(c)(3)
nonprofit organization, and we rely on public support to carry
out our mission of publishing extraordinary work that may be
outside the realm of the large commercial publishers. Financial
donations are welcome and are tax deductible.

for Mark Emile Sanjay
and Emily Jane Anjani

CONTENTS

From country to country you wing,
each branch a bulbul's perch
you will forsake come morning.

Where does my heart belong?

—BHOJPURI FOLKSONG

THE
COWHERD'S
SON

THE COWHERD'S SON

O Krishna, O flautist,
> what thrill to wind another's flute!
To have fingers guide air,

> stop its prayer leaking from holes
plugged with pads and mantras.
> My prayers are hollow

reeds or shells whose mollusks
> I've fricasseed. My love tasted of sea
and relics: the tooth of Gautama,

> the finger of the Baptist,
locusts and wild honey. For its music
> I punch gaps into his femur

and press this flute to my lips
> to Pied Piper Hindu twinks
in Queens out of bikini briefs.

> I mix rum in my milk and we suck
spirits down all Saturday night
> and *Jai Jagdish Hare* Sunday morning.

O Kanhaiya, O Madhav,
> My father Ahiri, my mother Brahmin
now Christian carnivores.

> Mixed-caste and queer-countried,
I'm untouchable, the only Mohabir left
> who still scores your shlokas.

HOLI LOVESPORT

I.

We two drunken roses
Chests in ruby play swirl
Holi in south Queens my lover
Has many faces I know

II.
The Cowlord rumbles, the sapphire
hurricane of Yaduvansh rumbles.

The cowherds' dandiya lovesport
pichkariya paint vermilion drama:

a ballad map back to that sacred forest.
Their tears: one thousand moon shards.

Krishna cavorted with all the maids:
the gopiya painted an emerald monsoon.

In their tear-ducts, jealousy's pearls
he wears as studs in his ears.

III.
Aunties slur behind fingers,
churn milky whispers solid
to shame me into Diaspora.

Raven oceans from India,
this cowherd boy, sings kajari
love songs for that flautist.

Abi lef da side lang time
Til now you na get sense.

IV.
In Yayati's home, I leave my arms and good
name at father's feet, take up flute, tie rope

in raga, from cow to my own new name.
Multicolored love drops. A seven-hued bow

shoots holy joy across our bodies bound by
this principle. A slur. A thunderous love,

I am of Krishna's line.

V.

My lover covers coy smiles

    with a coral dawn dupatta.

We untuck our silk corners;

    sail citrine souls to honey-wood,

dance full maroon gibbous,

    the abir in sandal and jasmine.

VI.
There in finger-strokes I paint
dusk on his riverbank,
but he had already stained
my whole body.

A BODY OF MYTHS

In a night cell, you are half
man half woman. My father

chases us into the wood, crying out
for blood, sickle-handed,

the forest's roots flailing their limbs like asps.
I give you my name.

Can your papa count
my fingers as kin *forever and ever?*

Don't melt his ears, Lord Shiva, it's my goat head,
a goat head hungry for fig leaves.

Shame, shame, shame! I know your —
In Union Square a kiss betrays . . .

not to a crest of thorns, but to a hail of fists.
Anywhere I chase the mango-sun

to jaw it whole is crowned
in blood with no chance of resurrection.

TOUCH ME NOT

Son, you are fit
                    only for the greasy smoke
of the body burning on its pyre,
                    of women's hair and liars' teeth.

You can't apologize
                    for a lowly birth,
this sea you must cross on a craft
                    with your own lashed bones.

Fool, you have not given me
                    a son's gift, nor caressed
a woman's breast as a field
                    that will feed for generations.

You can't arrest the blood
                    vessel mid sea. I could wait
one thousand years for you
                    to jettison

the plough's iron weight,
                    a woman's swollen belly over the bow.
But you are an imposter, suckled
                    at a dead heifer's teat,
                            a Hepatitis crow,

a blight on this line, dropped
                    in the stable eating
vulture meat and spreading disease.
                    You've refused me your youth

and for this, my palace will torment you
                    with rubies you bleed
when thorns prick your quick.
                              When men ask

to which mount you belong,
                    you will look at their palms,
your own hands stiff
                              with cow shit stoking a pyre-flame.

VIVAH AT THE DURGA TEMPLE

for Akta Kaushal

Draupadi, did you take all five brothers
at once, each man squeezing the Mount Meru

of the other man's nipples in excitement?
India was inscribed on your skin. When

Duryodhan pulled your silk did it prophesy
Sanskrit's own unraveling; the partition

of desire by seen and unseen?
The Shiv Sena will assassinate me for saying

Arjun let Krishna drive his chariot,
you know what I mean. But what of your choice?

Brahmins malign you for their own myopia.
Were you between the brothers at night or

veiled, did you slide down the balcony and
into the tongue of Lalita's holy fire?

RELIEF

But now, drought. My body
is a starving night. I've tried

every incantation's glide, every
folk-remedy; thrown ash

of torn clothes from the cliff
to salt clouds—

I have no herb left to burn. No
scorpions to jewel a curse,

no rattlesnake to drape
from my neck. Far off

you hurricane; a mountain emeralds,
a drowned doe bloats. I bite

my lip and mouth
your name. A vulture whirls

from my throat in a violet bloom.
You, the omen of flashflood:

first rapture, then raptors.

PAPER LANTERN

for Gangadai Mohabir

The spirits gather at my doorstep;
all day I storm. Downtown, they light boats
of bamboo and rice paper
to blow over the ocean.
On top of the ridge at Kuliʻouʻou
someone etches your name
into a picnic table though
she doesn't mean you. Ganga,
you are now rain:
when your hands no longer reached,
your daughter chopped off your bun.
The river shares your name,
looses her own silver silt into the ocean;
in this way all seas are Ganga,
and you are all water.
I light a match to inspire
this bamboo offering
until the flame unwinds its coils to wisps
of white hair. I set hope alight
inside when sailing your story
and cut through saline breaks.

COOLITUDE

The Ganges are not our holy waters.
— Andil Gosine

You ask me to bring a lota of brass
for your sun prayers. I hold out my hands
to you cupped, dripping every Hudson drop
you entrusted me. Silver moons breaking
into flight: the lift of sunrise plovers.
This is my favorite story. To tell you,
You are an estuary, I don't need
to read your palms. My own heart beats brackish
with your heart. Like kalapani meeting
the Berbice River, you crest against my
tide in swells and my joy refuses
stillness as one body draws the other.
Simply put: between my clay and your bone
the rift is a mangrove twist of knotted myths.

INDENTURE

Brits distilled rum in coolie blood,
hardly a high tide secret:

they folded complacent flood-time money
into hijabs, madrasi rumal, and pagri

to keep the sting of saltwater out
of their eyes. Guyana side: the toil of cutlass,

hoe, and bhoosi-husk. Their children seed
today's fields with toothy ploughs:

false teeth, diabetes, white masks,
Mercedes, Rum and Coca Cola,

three-bedroom mortgages, 24-karat gold
eagle-bands, El Dorado and Johnny Black.

Drink up. Drink up. Drink up. Drink up. Drink up.

Let's see what blood recalls.

DIABETES PRAYER

Gods of cane, I too am bent before the grinder,
my tongue swollen and pasty.

Gods of cutlass and gashes unhealed,
a hymn exhales rests in the air; my stitches rip with each inhale.

I drape myself in a shroud,
my ox ribs riddled with fructose scars.

Some things I cannot control,
the son of a son of a slave.

I cavort with refined disaccharide lovers, stoned
on jilebi and rum.

God of indenture and addiction, I've hacked off my feet
and gouged out my own eyes to drink you.

In 1890 Lakshman's back blackened in a Skeldon field.
He bent your stalks into a temple and planted a frangipani tree

in the courtyard. Each flower, a phantom
of sugar, each flower a ghost of a prayer

he would forget. Cane flowers
gouged ravines in his forearms and bite

his children still. Gods of fair exchange, can I ransom
my own Demerara blood with toes and cut foreskin?

RUM AND COCA-COLA

We sit and suck rum whole night.
You're a brown boy in love with the USA
until the soldiers sneak into the logies,
snap the necks of peace-dollars.

Whiteness, Vitiligo of desires
that do not sleep until *Sanco chase*
he lovah from de dam into the river below.
But you can erase it Sanco, boy,

doesn't matter if you went to tie a goat
and cut the wrong throat, you can rub
it out in rum. If the police come
you will blend in if you wear red, white,

and pack your mouth with the gauze
of English, in pennies and "Morning,
Neighbah, Mahnin'." Sanitize your criticism
that leaves you without a cent in your palm;

your pockets holed, open mouthed
like children you sired. Your GI
tek dey eye an' pass 'em.
A-we hain't nuttin' but crab dogs.

BLIND MAN'S WHIST

Play your hand of loss, in fact,
        your deck was glass, now
it's in slivers. Any cutlass deal
        will cost an eye. Think of it:
your color is the One-eyed Jack's,
        either a spade or red-skinned
after the sun's molten gold casts
        you into a new caste. You are sick
of being broken, every metaphor
        for you is one of soldered pieces,
a wistful colony-memory of a once
        promised return: a 19th-century
pirate game you learned in the dark,
        taught by your father: suicidal
king wagering your mother's gold
        teeth for a trick and re-signing
an indenture contract that forfeits
        return passage for this Skeldon paddy
field. The gamble is you never see
        your own assets, you try to drown
yourself in rum, stuffing English
        into your mouth and still allow
magistrates to fill you with silence.
        Guyana was called El Dorado
because of the promise of gold,
        but it was empty. El Dorado
is a promise of rum, that soon
        your hand will trump all others,

and you will clear the table with one
        knock from your arm and pull
your brothers up to dance while one
        selects a chantey from the jukebox
and another hacks a settlement in the corner.

EL DORADO, 1998

The country hath more quantity of gold, by manifold,
than the best parts of the Indies, or Peru.
— Sir Walter Raleigh

Follow the beach down the Corentyne
saturated with the runoff of Khan's saw mill
upstream from 59 village to Baba Grant,
over a small footpath bridge.
Crabwood Creek dries into a chasm
of human waste, animal refuse, and flies.
The road ends in jungle cows
and missionaries. All along the banks
of the Corentyne, smoldering
pyres and half-burned driftwood
of Crabwood float. Even this flotsam
is unable to trace a path to the open sea
to ride the nexus of north and south
equatorial currents. When the river recedes,
garlands of marigolds and dead fish
bake in the sun until the brown waters
rise again to claim their ghosts. There,
in a house on stilts, overlooking the river,
the senile aunty drinks cream soda,
the clear one made mostly of cane,
bleached the color of the smiling
white woman on the Demerara sugar
billboards so white it wouldn't know how
to cast a shadow. The auntie's mother
stepped off the boat and cleared a path
from the Skeldon Estate to Crabwood Creek,

a village settlement of coolies freed
of their contracts. She unties a makeshift
pouch from her lace orhni.
Earned from labor in the sun, the death
of her only son to diabetes and El Dorado Select,
an inheritance: three copper coins
from India she calls dachna.

BULBUL

for Atin, Mae, and Bulbul

Who tied you to a perch
to carry you to market? Gold
cannot hold the sun that blazes

your furcula. You wish
for wings in this life of heartbreak.
What cruelty for your maker

to stir such music inside your chest:
a winged honey to warble
while you weep, your foot

tied to a stick. Not even the song
in your throat is yours though
mustered from your cage

of sinew and bones. Crows,
koyals, dwijahs alike steal
every grain from your beak.

SITA

Sita signed her sentence with a thumbprint. That morning
she filled a lamp with mustard oil to keep burning until
she came back. The arkotiya, recruiter for the East India
Company, dressed as a wandering ascetic. He begged at her
door. He hypnotized her with coins in the shape of a deer.
He bared his ten demon heads, demanding her memory. Sita's
eyes glowed gold.

Held at the Kolkata shipping dock, the first sea she would
know, Sita sat on a chariot bound for the City of Gold.
Her junglee children were yet to run through the Amazon,
barefoot. Cutlass mangled eye and limb, chopped India out
of *coolie*, a new word for her labor. She cried for the hart
that betrayed her. Her Skeldon calluses hardened into a
Guyana map.

Every night Sita's dream flickered. She saw herself changed
by the black seas. Every night Sita dreamed an India that
did not want her back. The golden stag glinted, fleeing
deeper into the forest.

TEMPLE IN THE SEA

In Trinidad, when the British outlawed
        temples, Siewdass ripped
open his chest—
        his own flesh, unruled. Jailed

for his shrine to the monkey god
        on Tate and Lyle's field,
his mandir would no longer tremble,
        would tear its indenture contract.

In 1947 he leapt across the kalapani—
        Every day he gathered stones
from the fields in his bag,
        rode to the Gulf of Paria,

walked five hundred feet
        from shore, piled the stones until
a mountain rose. As if to reclaim
        something lost, did the stones

themselves help by refusing to sink?
        Siewdass once carried an entire mountain
for hundreds of miles
        on his left hand to revive

the destitute, the servants marooned
        in cane fields bluing
from drinking slavery's poison.

ODE TO RICHMOND HILL

then the drunk teen scatters
a cascade of copper on cement,
the old Uncle yells, eyes silver
with disbelief, *Pick up yuh*
paisa, na man! no worry
on this slate day youths dem
speak no Hindi to know *paisa*
means *money*, a taxi speeds by
blaring a chutney remix of
Kaise Bani and you remember
your Aji dropping her rum
at Aunty's party to jump up
and your mother's awkward Hindi—
you bit your fingers with each roti
she rolled, each mantra she taught you
floods your throat in front
of this puja shop front on 127th
and Liberty strung with plastic marigolds,
a replica strung of polypropylene
like you are now and not like
long time when Par-Aja came
from India, you are a forgery
that will one day burn
not on a pyre but in an incinerator,
not on a riverbank, but
in a crematorium, your prayers
in Hindi accented in English alveolars
neither devas nor prophets
recognize as supplication
but on Liberty Avenue
in the waft of a spliff drag,

and sandalwood a coolie Uncle
in a kurta mouths Marley
as you walk by
you start to sing praise
to Queens where you are
Chandra's son or so-
and-so's buddy ke pickni,
where you wipe oil from doubles
on your jeans and cuss up
the car that backs into stacked crates
of strawberries, to where you
return after three years
and Richmond Hill opens
its coolie arms, pulls you close,
and in your ear whispers,
dis time na long time.

WOUND

I give you a mockingbird's skull
sealed in a glass jar; the sun

crescendos until its story flowers
then dries into dust and feathers.

It shocks me to dream my body
as a cut pomegranate. From my skin

rubies slip, vibrant in arid air
pluming into tanagers, branch-fallen

fledglings that toe to their nest
of woven waste; you, a deer wandering

into my score of chirps, with one mouth-
breath chew my hatchling bones

to usher your sprouts into full horn. Your throat
is the tributary of visceral trumpeting,

a yellow fire I once mocked, though,
you feed me red too. You're not alone. I hunger

to tongue your every seed, to make certain
your water is storm first, then river.

A PRAYER AT NAURAAT

Mother,
       I hold the clay lamp until
my fingers are tongues of flame
that scribe in soot. I am smoke

that's never stopped curling. See
what smolders in the field,
cane, toil, or the corpse of colony.

Mata,
       I have left again across the sea
you'd never dream was mapped, I am
even farther from India than you.

Amma,
       In Hawai'i a poet eats lava
stones to resist genocide. Meanwhile
the Japanese set up towers and dance
the electric slide. We children
of the sea swell with memory.

Your image on my bookshelf is a mirror
you visit to see the marks
on your face painted vermillion.

Are you behind those paper eyes?

My mother's saris from her mother
are folded into creases. The silk
disappears thread by thread, like
the India ink on Aji's forearm
as she wrinkled and split at the seams.

Ma,

       I've swallowed the whole sea
and again I am from somewhere new,
again I am disappearing.

Devi,

       If I light the lamps will you find me?

DEEPAK RAGA

Look at the darkness in your temple.
What words will spark your fuse,
huzur?

Don't smash the clay lamps.
Tear back the skin in my forearm
and pluck its saffron tendons—

Open your throat and the gourd you cradle
leaps into flicker.

Sienna finches flit from lips to wick.
I catch one glowing ember and
swallow it whole.

Subhanallah! against the marble walls.
I am your tambura.

You sear your fingertips
against my river veins.

BUTCHERING A HEN

after Ross Gay

First pull the breast
up from the legs until
the hollow echoes
the bone's scrape
on steel and tear
apart the ribs and hips
cartilage snapping and
by then the plastic wrap
will drip in syrup
that's not quite blood
but a diluted death
that opens its maw or begs
for the shreds of fat and skin
I have learned to not
render into the ache
of an artery
or another indenture story—
Sabu's stallion galloping
across the sky, Ala ad-Din's
Persian or Mowgli's elephant
this vessel of curry will taste
like eating sandalwood coals
stinking of the Orient
but not the Orient
of Jalal ad-Din nor of Kabirdas,
who as I understand it
was all woof and wool
and even worse:
a vegetarian, instead of chanting
any name, I'd rather tear

the flesh of a bird
like the banyan does,
roots eating stone and corpses
of the mynahs that congregate
crowding evening with their salah
and tantra-mantras,
my own hands my mother's
hands knobby, a mango
wood *bismillah* like Lala's
Madras Curry Powder
or my mother's mother's knuckles,
Ammamma orphaned
with Muslim and Hindu earrings
like water stirred into milk,
mixed in Chennai a ghost
now frying in Oviedo, Florida,
hungry for pink flesh
and her mother's name
now a flame-licked pot
and now a slow boil
something unremembered
that still stings and burns
and blindly, I tear the roti
and sop up what pools
with oil stewed into something new,
tearing muscle from bone,
my fingers smeared
with pepper sauce

YOUR MOTHER PRAYS IN THE METROPOLITAN MUSEUM OF ART

Dear mother's mother's mother,

I wend the labyrinth of my mitochondrial chambers
amidst the art stolen from temples and

I have found you here though
I no longer speak Tamil,

and I feed my daughter beef.

Dear Brahmin, dear jahajin who has no name
other than these teeth,

if I have dishonored you by leaving my husband
to drown himself in rum and women,

I am not sorry.

O Devi—O Mata, it's you who asked her mother
to open her jaws—to devour her wholly.

O Ma, in this hall it's I who open my mouth.

MANTRA

O gods of ash,
I have found you and am not of you.

This mask of clay will smash
against the river stones and I will sail
Snow Moon into the pollution of years

of broken sutras, a wreckage
of browned marigolds at the throats of used-up
idols and burnt-out clay lamps.

O gods of brass. O gods of burns
then sandalwood paste,

hear me. I was once as you are. Fixed
to a base or brushed in camel hair,
lips parted, prayers caught
as vireos in my throat.

O clay gods, o gods of phase,
may you singe your own sky.

O gods of today, of broken things,
some things misplaced where they belong;
gristle and shell fall away.

A macaw flies from its cage
in midtown Manhattan, unaccustomed to sky:
a rainbow streak.

HOLI

for Robindra Deb

Coward, how can you warm your hands
so far from the Holika in flames?

Come closer and trace the subway and ship
lines in these palms. You gather embers

in your dustpan to light your own fire
and dream of the return of some god

who will pull you from this coolie history
unscathed, who will tear out

the slaver king's intestines and garland
his neck in pink entrails. Somewhere

outside a Ram temple someone smashes
a mirror and places the shards in her mouth.

Cowherd, can you pray, your tongue
so cleft, or do you eat the coals

to cauterize the mantras flapping
wild as cicadas in your hollow?

Look around at beauty cloaked
in orange. Everything you love

will one day burn.

LIGHT THE CITY

The match　　　　spits
　　　flame

　　　　　　　　to blacken the lamp's
　　　　　　　　　　　river clay.

Earthen pots
　　　overflow.

　　　　　　　Gold in four directions

tongues the city
　　　until the clay cracks

　　　until the wick
　　　　　　vanishes—

A Diwali diya
on the October windowsill,

this body
　　　　slowly

　　　　　　　　　　burns.

COW MINAH: AJI TELLS A STORY

Ek-go

Bahut pahile ke bat hai. Ek-go rajah rahi aur okar haal bahut bura rahi. So come so done. Lang time day, da king been a-sick bad-bad, an a-sickness dem ojha man cyan cure.

One Ahir, a cow minah name Ramlall been a-mine cow. 'E been keep 'em and take 'em one one time fa graze a-pastua. Ahir na been da? You know how dem ahir stay an wha kine wuk dem a-do? Dem a-mine cow fa de milk and dem dus mek pera, barphi, an so. So dis Ramlall been mine gai an ting.

Aur aapan gaiyan ke khetwa me charawat charawat ek mitti awaj sunal. Aur ii surela awaj ek-go larki ke rahi. Etni mitti. 'E been a-walk a-pastua an tek 'e cow dem fa graze. An when 'e put 'e foot doung pon a-saft mud 'e hear one naise. An ova sweet baice wha been sing so,

> *Ahirwa Ahirwa haddi pe na kuchale*
> *ohar gulab lutke bhaiya hamke mare hai.*
>
> *Cow Minah, Cow Minah, na mash me bone*
> *me brodda kill me yondah side an tek me*
> *flowah rose.*

❧

This is how it happened. Long ago a king had an illness no doctor could cure.

A cowherd named Ramlall kept cows and would take them to graze in the pasture. He was of the Ahir caste, you know what work they do? They keep cows for milk and make sweets.

One day while Ramlall was watching his cows, he stepped on the soft earth and heard a sweet voice sing,

> *Cow Minder, Cow Minder, don't mash my bones*
> *my brother killed me over there and took my rose.*

Dui

*Me papa been ge sick an call a-ojha man come tek 'e pulse fa
janchwa karawe see wha wrong wid 'em. Da ojha man been
check an poke an mash up he skin all about like fa help 'em but
no body na know wha wrong wid 'em.*

*One day me papa been dream 'e dream. 'E dream 'e been de in
a-bush wid one lota watah an den 'e go pray a-de Durga mandir
wha dem banbasi been mek. 'E talk 'e mantra dem an tek 'e lota
an offah 'em to one tree wha been de de. An in 'e dream whe 'e
pour de watah one lal gulab stat fa grow. De red red rose been
smell so sweet da when da king smell 'em okar haal teak bhail.*

*An me papa call all me buddy dem, me brodda dem Jujistir,
Arjun, Bhim, Nakul, Sahadeo, and Bahadur fa come cana whe
'e de an 'e been say who-sor-evah find de flowah must come gi
'em, an 'e go mek 'em rajah. So come so done. One day me been
a-go a mandir fa pray ke me papa go de good, and aftah aarthi
utawe me been a-go peepal ke perwa fa pani charawe. When
watah been spread on a-groung me see dis red red rose grow.*

*Ham ii sochat rahi ke ii phoolwa hamar baba ke jaan ke
bachaibe. Me tink dis must be da devi phool wha go mek me
papa de good.*

⸘

*My father was sick and called the doctors to diagnose him; all
were unable.*

*One night my father dreamed that he went to the jungle with
a pot of water to pray at the goddess's temple made by the forest*

dwellers. He offered the water to a nearby tree. When he poured it, a sweet-smelling rose grew from the moistened earth. This flower healed him.

My father sent for all of my brothers, Jujistir, Arjun, Bhim, Nakul, Sahadeo, and Bahadur, saying that he would coronate whoever finds this rose. One day I went to the temple to pray for my father's recovery and I offered the water to a peepal tree. Where the water hit the earth, a red rose started growing.

I knew this was the goddess' flower, the one to save my father's life.

Tin

Hear Bahadur tak, "Bahin, o bahin, tohar haath me ka ba?
Wha de in you han, sista?"

Me giyam answa, "Bhaiya ham devi ke paas puja kare gaili aur
ii phulwa paayli. Buddy, me been go pray a-Durga mandir an
me fine a-flowah-dis. Come le abi-two tek 'em an gi daddy."

But me buddy been get bad mine and seh "Chalo bahini, chalo.
Abi dis bhai-bahin go tek a flowah and gi abi daddy so 'e go
come good." *An 'e tek out a-talwar, a-cutlish 'e been cerry and
chop me pon me neck an shouldah an belly until me bleed an
bleed an bleed an all me ladri pitch out an hai bhagwan mar
gaili!*

*An 'e tek me shav and bering me in dis fiel ya-so. 'E been gi me
papa de flowah an me papa say 'e go come king afta 'e dead, 'e go
abhisek 'em like.*

*Le wo, ahirwa, le wo, hamar badan ke haddi. Tek dis, cow
minah, tek dis, me han ke bone go show all body dem whe 'e been
firs chop me. Hamar gaana aapan haddi mein bhi hojai! Sab
logan ke samne ham aapan ganwa gaaib! An me song wha de
inside me han ke bone go sing in front a-all body.*

§

Bahadur said, "Sister, what's in your hand?"

I replied, "Brother I went to pray at the goddess's temple and
found this flower. Come, let's go give it to father."

45

But my brother had already made up his wicked mind, "Come, sister, come let both of us take this flower to father so he may be healed." *He took out his sword and pierced my stomach, hacking me limb from limb until I bled to death.*

He brought my remains to this field and buried me here. He gave my father the flower, and my father gave Bahadur his blessing. Bahadur will be installed as king after my father passes.

Take this, cowherd, my bone from my arm. It stores my song where he first cut me. Take my bone and go to my father's house. I will sing it so they all will hear.

Chaar

Maha rajah jai ho! Cow Minah tek out a-bone wha de inside 'e
pagri and put 'em in 'e han an rub 'em an a-bone stat fa sing.

> *Papa, o papa na mash me bone!*
> *Bahadur hamke mareke phulwa luta hai.*
>
> *Papa, o papa na mash me bone!*
> *Bahadur kill me yondah side an teef me flowah*
>   *rose.*
>
> *Papa, o papa na mash me bone!*
> *Bahadur kill me yondah side an teef me flowah*
>   *rose.*

ʓ

May you live long, my king! The cowherd took out the bone
he hid in his turban and started to stroke it. The bone started
singing.

> *Papa, o papa don't mash my bones!*
> *Bahadur killed me in the field and stole my rose.*
>
> *Papa, o papa don't mash my bones!*
> *Bahadur killed me over there and stole my rose.*
>
> *Papa, o papa don't mash my bones!*
> *Bahadur killed me over there and stole my rose.*

Paanch

Rajah tek a-flowah an show Bahadur. 'E tell 'em, *Smell a-flowah dis. Dis a-you sistah self! Dis Devi-Mata self self! Smell 'em you rakshas!*

An 'e tek one step mo close to Bahadur. 'E point a-flowah pon Bahadur ke face an Bahadur stat fa friken. An 'e face come mash up mash up. Da flowah been so nice Bahadur been cyan bear fa look. 'E been real neemakharam, real bad kine people.

'E eye start fa turn black an come lil lil. 'E skin stat fa tighten an tear near 'e mouth. 'E face turn like a jumbie an 'e stat fa rotten an dead out so. 'E stat fa renk nasty nasty. O god-o, how da renk full up da whole dehaat!

Aisan bhaile ke bhai-bahin mar gaile aur rajah ke okar yaad aike ta ro paral. So come so done, two bahin-bhai, buddy and sistah all two dead out an how rajah miss 'e pickni dem an stat fa cry an cry.

The king took the flower and showed Bahadur. *Smell this flower, this is your sister. This is the goddess! Smell it you rakshas!*

He took one step closer to Bahadur and put the flower in his son's face. Frightened, Bahadur's face started to decompose. Bahadur was unable to bear the flower's beauty.

His eyes started to turn black and shrink. His skin started to tighten and tear at the corners of his mouth. His face started to dry out. This is how he died. He started to rot. The smell of his rotting flesh spread across the whole country.

This is how it happened. A brother and sister both died and the king mourned their loss.

MYNAH

for Roger Sedarat

The quarrelsome bird is a poet named *mynah*.
His tongue roves the world over, this homeless mynah.

Kanchan stole Popo's songs we dance to in London.
For his each coolie chord she instead struck a minor.

In her Brampton project Aji dreamt of Guyana,
her bones sown in a field like the story "Cow-Minah."

Me aunty na wan know de antiman nephew
who like Manna Dey sing "O Meri Maina."

In Mānoa, a Hawaiian woman says to a white one,
"Haoles are haoles, no such thing as *kamaʻāina*."

ambergris sirf eke jagah ki nahin.
barf pighale kiska chehera dikhaye aina?

       (Ambergris is not only of one place.
       When ice caps melt whose face is in the mirror?)

Cast off, Paul Raimie Rajiv Mohabir, your each name a ship-
scrape, the horizon entices and your moorings are minor.

MY NAME IS A MAP

I. PAUL PRAYS AS A CHILD:

Dear God of my father only,

Forgive me for my sins,
even the ones I can't remember.
Pap says all my ancestors burn
in Hell because the British didn't baptize
their souls before they died.
I don't want to think that my Nani
and Nana are still afire because
he was a pandit and she converted
from Emma Louisa to Amla Devi,
and my Aja too, who began to name
his five sons after the Pandu brothers,
who sent his children to the missionaries
so that they could learn the British
ways though he himself was still a Hindu.
Thank you for erasing Pap's
sins with baptism, washing him
with the blood of the lamb,
and for calling him Richard.
He says I'm lucky to be named Paul
because no one will ever suspect
I am brown when I fill out papers
or speak on the phone. Paul is a mask
that Saul from the Bible used
after the scales fell from his eyes
on the road to Damascus.
Paul is my costume too
so that no one will treat me differently,
like a second-class citizen.

O God, wash me in your holy blood
and make me look like the Southern Baptists;
make me white and clean and
I will never stop serving you.

II. RAIMIE

A coolie's escape from the colony
to the metropole's grace signifies growth
of character. Laborers no longer
wash their asses with water and hands, but
are *Indian in color and British*
in taste. Mom and Pap ran off to Croydon,
dinner parties and extravagance far
from the poverty they knew. Why not be
opulent, spit in the plantation's eye?
Yet every Londoner discerned their dark-
skinned secret. So none would call me "Paki,"
they gave me an English name to render
me illegible; my name is a map,
a nautical chart of my displacement.

iii. Rajiv Lochana: A Ghazal in Translation

How is Ganga-jal pure when its human filth blinds
every creature that moves beneath its silt?

From the murky slime at the bottom of the lake
the lotus grows, petals unstained by dirt.

Ram's eyes are blue lotuses: cool though tumult
terrorizes you, abandons you in the forest.

In India I sat before a pandit in Vishwanath temple,
he wanted my name, jati, gotra, and nakshatra:

Rajiv, Gwalbans Ahir, Chandravansi, Pushya,
to offset my London birth with Allahabad Ganga-jal.

Given my nakshatra, star sign, my name should start
with "Ho" but I bear the sin of never fitting,

a Chandala, bound to wear iron for a Shudra father
and a Brahmin mother, but to be queer too—

he blasphemes, he who crawls into another
man's bed to peel the lotus for its seed.

IV. MOHA- VS. MAHA-

Mahabir uu bandarwa ke nam hai
je kalapani ke paar kudke urdal

The name of Lakshman's son became my last,
as per custom. He rose up, a great warrior,

to protest the magistrate's white prick raping
his wife while he cut cane midday in the Skeldon field.

Before pens and paper, letters were the same
as buffalo. Sons took their fathers' first names

as their last. Somewhere on the sugar plantation
a mistake was carved into heirloom: an "o"

in the place of "a"; greatness traded for
seduction. This explains too much:

why my Aja married three women and why
I may have family in Berbice I've never met.

> *Mahabir is the monkey's name,*
> *who took flight and crossed the black seas.*

MYSTERIOUS ALEMBICS

for Sarah Stetson

On the grass beneath my favorite tree, pecans surprise the back, the calf, the skull when napping in the plaza. The Hari Krishna girls sit next to me. A lesbian in a dinosaur t-shirt and her fag ask me to make bracelets out of grass. *Is this from your country?* No from Chuluota, about one hundred miles away, Mvskoke for tall pines.

❧

On Park Street, on Mother Theresa Road, an ascetic prods the topography of my right palm. I lie about my caste so he will touch me. He tells me in two months, when I return to the United States from Kolkata, I will marry a white woman. This marriage will mirage. Two months afterward, I will marry again for good, a Desi girl. *Ek lakh lakh pardesi girl.* She will make daal like my mother.

❧

Castes brought to Guyana by the British 1838–1917: Kahar (servant), Ahir (cowherd), Chamar (leather worker), Kshatriya (warrior), Brahmin (priest), Chandal (body burner), Mussalman (Muslim), Christian, Mali (gardener), Julha (Muslim weaver), Kurmi (farmer), Koiri (weaver), Thakur (landowner), Nai (barber), Dhobi (washerman), Dosadh (watchman).

❧

Gainesville. I live with my cousin. He's not actually my cousin. His great-great-grandfather and my great-grandfather were on the same boat from Kolkata to Guyana. His parents converted to Arya Samaj. *Dharti, agni, jal, pavan,* the elements—there is only om. He doesn't let me hang my om tapestry. *American Hindus just don't get it.* I'd eaten Orientalism for breakfast that day.

ॐ

A child in front of the Durga-Kund basti in Varanasi crouches, naked. He squats. He shits a soup of watery daal. A puppy licks the trail on the road made of compacted dirt. *These people live with infection.* If you die in Varanasi, you will escape rebirth. *I don't order daal when I go to the restaurant.*

ॐ

The sun sets on the dune with Dhiraj Mahraj, the brahmin who owns the camels we ride. I breathe deeply. *USA mein parha-huwa aadmi kyu bharat aaya hai.* His village is close. *Bhai-sahib, come talk with the old men. They are asking who is meditating on the dunes at sunset.* The Thar dusk: I see antelopes painted pink-orange and in shadow stretch across the desert. *Is the USA as far as Pakistan?*

ॐ

Daal recipe in three generations, masoor daal, onions, garlic, peppers, tumeric, cumin, garam masala, curry leaves, mustard seeds, salt, black pepper, cloves, black cardamom. Half masoor, half urad, Aji calls me Chandal. I call my grandmother from

Queens and record her voice telling me how to make daal. I do the same with my mother. The best I can figure is that I like chunks of tomatoes, quartered. Immokalee, where the tomato farmers struggled with slave wages, was close to where I grew up.

≀

Today I admit that I didn't know the prayers for bathing in the Ganges river. *It's Ganga-ji.* There aren't grassy knolls in Jackson Heights; I haven't married an Indian woman. Don't think that'll happen.

BOUND COOLIE

In the Guiana cane fields, it was commonplace
for a man to turn to another man,

to loosen his baba and to stare at the clouds
race across the sky, especially in the rainy months,

I expect—those kajari months of *my lover
lives in which country*—the truth is

that there were few women to caress
bound bodies—the truth is queerness

was a tool for survival, a trade wind to sail a kite
then cut its cotton string. I imagine

the cane fields, the foliage teeth burned
away, blackened, dotted white in strewn

dhotis and pagris of men, inside
men's mouths and fingers—

like on the platform where one night
in Fort Hamilton I waited

for a Queens-bound F train to open baleen;
to swallow me like krill when I knelt

before the Trini dread and he sky-gazed
dreaming of Chaguanas and frigate birds

only to see the crash and the spark of
the metal rails inside Brooklyn's belly.

THE RIVER-SON'S BETRAYAL

Ganga, the river goddess,
        drowned her seven sons as infants.
When the Vasus were still

        unborn she vowed to release them
from their mortal forms before
        she pretended to be human

and married a king who swore
        to never question her. I too pretended
much for my mother's sake,

        buried secrets in silt;
swallowed tumult of the adolescent
        thrill of wrestling the other boys

in our neighborhood. At night
        we kept our windows unlocked;
come morning, I tucked shame

        in my braids as milkweeds
and fairy wands, myself a wild flower.
        The king broke his promise

and stayed his wife's murderous hand.
        She returned to the blind dolphins
and perched atop a gharial.

        The son ripened and his body
betrayed him to its flood.
        Did she make a compact before

she made my body from her clay?
      Would my father have tried to drown
me in the baptismal font,

      himself, if he knew
some sons won't be damned?

BISMILLAH

If you want a poem that obeys
the strictures of doha and dactyl,

then I am unlettered. A crab dog
from backdam and bush shaping

cane into couplet. What do I know
of convention, my father a cowherd

my mother maharajin. The prophet ascended
the heights of verse when the Almighty stoked

fire in his blood. Recite. Recite.
Tell me in rhyme, of this turmoil within

that sears Jibril's whisper into
the pith of this body.

FALL

Every mass draws every mass. Our
book of hours: you on the beach

overlooking Mokulēʻia where you,
sun-burned, cast the hunger

that caused you to sin into the sea.
An angel once rushed to open

the book of thirst and my salt tumbled
into abyss. Gravity is worth

the fall. I lay you on the altar
before you part your red lips

and with *Ave maris stella*—
declare praise for the Star of Sea.

Before you I lay a feast of fallen fruit.
I blow the ram horn. Our prayers crash

wave on sand until our chapel shakes.
Today I starve for you. Tomorrow

crows will pick all we leave behind.

CHAMBER MUSIC

Press me. Strings cut
your index, middle, ring
fingers and hum.

I yield and release
feral music caught in your strum.

Hold me. Smash the gourd
of my sitar. Fire roosts
in such flare.

Watch me stoke a concerto in your bones,

you say and finger
my ribs as violin strings arching
Bach across my fretless

neck, sheet music fluttering
in a fit—

a dove's black eyes: quarter then
sixteenth notes; along
my score, tanagers lift

into sudden aria.

MALHAR RAGA

You fill a copper urn with kush grass, a pile of rice, and
　　garlands of marigolds.

In all four directions, ghosts with quicksilver bellies crowd
　　the sky.

Mercurial, you salaam me, sickle in hand to slit my strings at
　　the bridge.

I slip into dream through the cotton shroud—redline into the
　　underworld at 103rd and Broadway.

I dip a flower in the Vaitarna River and touch it to my two
　　eyes. It turns into thunder.

The rains begin.

I dip a leaf into the river and it scales into a koyal's black
　　plume.

Silver glints in a flurry of moons, the rains begin.

The bird in monsoon pinions warbles my name with your
　　larynx and the rains begin.

I open my throat and swallow billows of cloud.

With a stick I write in the sand, *My Chandal love with the hole in your throat, it's hard not to lick your sores.*

CHANGE

The henna leaf betrays its red
        to brown. Dried, how can it say
to its lost blush, flushed with wine,

      your lips are home, as it scuffs
its edges along the cement,
        dragged by the chords of seasons?

There is no going back.
      Every word is a hole in the universe
where it should have been said,

      an echo or stillness filled by artists
and stargazers with Ecclesiastes.
      How can I tell you now, you are my home,

the wildfire crown of oaks or the tide
      of flame licking my veins?

HENNA

Why throw your bangles
in the river at all? Melt the gold
into a charm to keep you safe.
Henna is darkest before dawn
as mud that clings to the palm.
This is not a story of watermarks
or river lines. Your gold nose ring
has fallen amongst the reeds,
surely bringing shame to your family
should your in-laws tell your father.
What use is remorse when the leaf
will stain you in red anyway?
Tie your sari to your love's fabric.
Today everything you touch
turns to beauty.

GIFT FROM A GRANDMOTHER

for Tina Edan

She gave her granddaughter
        gold bangles so she
could escape a husband who,

        after drinking rum, snaps bones
and sinus cavities with curses
        curled as rum-fists that bruise

ears into believing the trap
        of words. Her own Aji
left her first husband

        to cross the sea and again
in Epiphany Village after
        the thrashing silence or

tumble down the stairs.
        There is no shame
in surviving anyhow you can,

        though your five sons
clutch their father's dhoti.
        I've always wished

for a crossroads, an option
        to buy my freedom,
to save my own hide

from the bear trap
set to spring its teeth
            into the boy's ankles who

does not run like the other boys
            after the basketball,
the boy who succeeds

            at every moment
in humiliating his father.

TUBERCULOSIS

An angel nests in your lungs
clawing holes into the pink,

toughened with cigarettes
and incense burned at midnight

for the dark gods. Your desire for silks
leaks from your prayers.

Your body is a colander. You remember
the little boy in the City of Light who

wipes his lips then stretches out hands
smeared in macabre, asking for one

or two rupees, who you reviled as he spoke,
de do, bhaiya, roti khila do, na.

You pull away, *Don't touch me!*
Will the seraphim pass him over,

his doorpost daubed with his own blood?
Who saved you then, the grandson of illiterate slaves?

Praise the god of Isoniazid,
his mercy renews each morning.

Your pipes betray and you think, *to pray is to beg.*
You are a flute to be tongued and fingered.

Play that bitter herb muic. Play
that thumri, the one where the angel's

feathers fall from your mouth.

A LETTER FROM NANA TO NANI

Ji,
I didn't mean to throw you down the stairs.

Back home, you sprouted pinions
and primaries and flew to eat the grains

from a Brahmin's hand, winging
from your poor life in the fields

to London's plundered leaf.

O jeera in my daal,
That day of Morning Prayer

did you fly from the body's door,
to forever break my skin with your beak,

to outline my sins against you—
or were yours the diaphanous wings

of the mosquito,
just outside the net at my ear

all night
keeping me from rest?

FADE

I.

Her silken or cotton skin at old age, brown and sun-cracked
       mud

India ink, curves of her husband's name tattooed on her right
       forearm

Pandit Hardowar with needles and coals, gouged letters into
       her skin—widows never remarry

Her husband wore a pink tunic and she a dandelion sari

Over time lightening into her skin, the spell of letters points
       towards Benaras

The Ganga floods its bank into rural wildflowers, into
       dysentery in cities

Fires dry her bones, sun the cobblestones

II.

Benarsi silk or Kolkota cotton on the handloom or by weft
       cards into one story, wrung out by dhobi hands,
       colors dye the water

Strung three years to dry, sometimes forgotten in a courtyard,
       or hung to admire the craft or the rainbow it lends to
       a household

Vermillion and olive tea the water, when squeezed splashing
    about the washer's feet, spring come early

The Lord of the Raghus plays Holi in Avadh, a crocodile
    stained the river with holy blood

Once the water retreats, how the fabrics blanche and crack
    into frayed fragments, wind and pleats and sunlight
    wear the body down

The threads, whether of stalk, whether of worm, slacken and
    curl as they snap, woven in Benaras or Kolkata,
    wherever worn, six yards by six yards

Kabir says, *in the end, your body burns into ash*

BACK-HOME GAMES IN FLORIDA

for Emile Mohabir

i. Kite

The smell of rubber cement and crepe paper; the sky in purple—

> A father splits bamboo skewers and glues them into
> an octagon.

*Back-home we'd use the paper stinking of the gilbaka and hourie
fish Ma'd bring back from Skeldon.*

> A father breaks his sacred thread.

*Back-home we soak the string in glue and glass before we sail
them into battle.*

> A father places the kite-thread in his son's hand.

*Back-home we gave them tongues that sang Hindi songs in the
sky.*

⸮

*—and how we'd cut down the neighbor boy's kite, two forms our
senior, and how his sister would smile at us as we'd walk down 'til
road-end. Back-home—*

> Somewhere a song waits to be carved into the sky.

Back-home after we cut down five kites, Madan put on the
white sheet and scared the pandit off his bicycle at midnight. He
chanted the Durga Kavach while waist-deep in the trench, his
dhoti soiled with piss and mud.

They enter the field. The kite does not lift like a
swallow from the son's hands.

ii. Bottle Caps

On the driveway Emile and I pound them into
disks—

Back-home, we'd sharpen the rim to cut each other's fingers to the
bone, and if we cut the opponent's cord too, then their disk was
ours.

    —hammer out moons of cement dust leave craters to
crouch.

The winners kept their spoils of disks and digits. But here, dis-
side, you cyan. You can't play how I played it. There are rules and
diseases here like tetanus and stitches.

With an awl Pap poled two holes in the middle of
each, strung them with cotton thread and spun—

Men don't know how to drink scotch and swear-screech Hindi
songs into the moonlight.

          and spun.

Men are so alone, and you will become wolves, hungry for a
hump and some meat. Here men fear intestinal worms from other
men's mud.

Behind the bungalow, Emile and I cut our teeth on
the whir of the spinning blade.

III. Leaf Seek

The whole of Skeldon to
        Baba Grant, Road End watch
                the halos of children, heads oiled

with coconut and moon,
        swaying like leaves in the salt-breeze.
                When the whole team bristles

against the fence of bent cane
        hear the next team,
                Aati-paati mango leaf—

—this side, who hides at night
        in back-home, nonsense? Brown
                boys in Chuluota are fewer

than mango leaves in the city.
        Aati-paati lime leaf—
                and all the coolie boys scatter

like crabs on the sea wall. It must get
        moonlight fa play. Backdam wall,
                koker, sluice gate, in cane fields,

in the jungle they hide until
        the seekers, bearing lime leaves jail
                them in the silver night. When you

catch a coolie babu by the longoti,
        gi' 'e rass one leaf and then hook 'em
                like ma catch hassa in the trench

with a stick, watch she does jook de wata.

STANDING ON A BRAMPTON DRIVEWAY
BEFORE THE SNOW

Rubber hums on pavement from the highway beyond the
        wooded area between houses.

Fifty-percent-off neon leaflet—newspaper insert, scrapes
        along the driveway.

Car alarm; drum and bass, cousin unlocks his car, slams door.

Idle chatter from front door crack: *the best coffee to wake up*
        to—

Roars of Caribbean laughter, clap-on-the-back thunderstorm.
        Uncles drink rum inside.

Door slam.

Three at a time, migrating ducks honk streaks in the sky.

Flakes blow east then fall to puddle on exposed skin.

Her body lies undressed on a cold metal drawer under
        halogens, I want her to wear the daffodil-yellow
        dress patterned in pink roses.

One starling lights on an oak branch, a single wind chime
        joined by another.

Slowly at first, starlings gain decibels, bloom like leaves, orchestrate black springtime.

Wind stirs like out-breath.

They leave one by one, the song diminishes, until the sound
of just one.

Then none.

HAUNTING

Every body is a haunted ruin: hinges
of bone and bone, and binds

grafting limbs into movement wearing down
like broken chandeliers and cathedral

stones. What echoes of prayer
are scrimshawed along the length

of femur and ulna that beg for *just this once*?
I only write you in loose friction.

Along ventricles, lights out,
you feel your way through

the sanctum into finality. At the basest stone
of your house you strike your foot

as you come in from rain. Your every step
away from our bed darkens

the thin fictions sliding between us.
In this building of shattered whispers

I say your words at night to taste you.

EMPTYING IN THE SEA

You tell me of a European machine
that removes filth from the Ganga.
If the river removes sin now,
what happens when the massive filters
produce a *cleaner* water—
all the submerged ashes, the black
fragments of bone of all those souls
will be exhumed, bagged and distributed
to landfills. Will they come back in echoes
of my grandmothers, those blue women
who tied *Devi* in the folds of their saris,
before they boarded ships docked
on that very river; ships named things like
the *SS Jura*, the *SS North*, and *HMS British Monarch*—
those dark women now wait to ferry us
to the next world. I used to scrub my skin hard,
to scour the brown until one day, fed up
with being dirty, always dirty, I washed
and washed until I wished for Hindi to swell
again in my mouth. You slide your fingers
down the current of my brown arm,
my mother asks if your eyes mimic the sea.
If they crash and foam, or if they are slate and still.
I hear the shipboards creak and splinter
in her throat. You say, *England is where you came*
to be free of that filthy river. I say,
The Thames is darker still, fouled with
loot, blood and black death.

DIRGE FOR KAMAL

It's late spring and the sun's joy
is a shadow.

             Dear Mami I never met,
this du'a is for my mother's grief.

        All morning she's stitch-ripped
the hem of her wedding sari's fall,

untied the knot of its pallu
from my father's dupatta

            that skirted her away from you
in seven steps.

She should have burned
its silk in the havan kund's sacred fire.

My mother's throat quivers
its farewells as mantras:

flaming dawn-
           arrows drawn, cascading

toward a house she built across the sea
with bricks of regret,
             a life spent

rent in two.

ORBIT OF EXTERIOR WILDFIRES

aag jo lagi samand mein, dhuan na pargat hoye
so jane jo jarmua, jaaki lagi hoye

The ocean aflame, the smoke is invisible.
Those who go close know its burn.
                                    — *Kabirdas*

When I open my eyes to red
my skin wants your finger,

sometimes four, sometimes to burn
in the gravity of our collision

where I swallow white light
and am silhouette, our mess dust

and offshoots of moon. Insatiable
I dream flames. I dream

erasure's rapture. I've spent
the lion-month gathering kindling

for this obeah fetish, this charm of bundled
deer-tongue, cubeb, damiana, hoping

some fever will leap again from you
a golden stag. I sing to you

a cremation lullaby—skulls crack
into script where fire ravages,

the spell scarred into a bowl
of bone, a tongue of closure.

UNWITTING PILGRIM

for Gaurav Mehra

You see florescent trucks
loaded with barefoot pilgrims,
smeared in white ash, Technicolor
red, blaring *hara hara mahadev shambo,*

arrive in the crisp chill
of Shivratri spring. You eat
ground *bhang,* shout *bole bham!*
Zoom past stores playing

the latest hit devotional song in Bhojpuri,
you dance in the street,
even though you cling to the back
of a motorcycle in heat, the cars

and honking busses kick up dust—
don't close your eyes to the lights.
Even though you reluctantly grasp
at the story of Ganga's fall to earth

carved into concrete, stained
gold and black, garlanded with strings
of marigolds (don't ask its meaning
expecting only one), don't shut

your eyes even if smears of sandal
fall from your forehead into your eyes, don't
shut out this flickering dance before you—
In fact, this city of light won't

be shut out. In fact, stop racing toward
contained closure in this open space
before you. In fact, stop reading; stop—

close your book right now.

"The Cowherd's Son" uses various names for Krishna and was inspired by "Confessions of a Would-Be Brahmin" by Sudesh Mishra and "The Cowherd" by Rooplal Monar. The words "*jai jagdish hare*" come from the aarti prayer of the same name, and they mean "*victory to the god of the universe.*"

"Touch Me Not" is based on the story of the king Yayati who exiled his son to the forest after stripping away his title and caste. Yadu, the prince, becomes a cowherd.

"Coolitude" is a concept developed by the poet Khal Torabully and the academic Marina Carter to chart the poetics of Indian indentures' diaspora. The poem's epigraph is from visual artist Andil Gosine's series "Our Holy Waters."

"Rum and Coca-Cola" is named after the Calypso song by the same title. This poem also draws on V. S. Naipaul's short story "Until the Soldiers Came." Some lines from this poem come from other Calypso and Caribbean folk songs, such as "Sanco Boy" and "Mahnin' Neighbah, Mahnin'."

"Blind Man's Whist" is based on a nineteenth-century card game.

"El Dorado, 1998": The epigraph is from Sir Walter Raleigh's *The Discoverie of Guiana* (1595).

"A Prayer at Nauraat" is a prayer at Navratri time and is meant as a prayer to the nine forms of the Goddess, all addressed as "mother." The poem refers to the Hawaiian song "Kaulana Nā Pua" ("Famous Are the Flowers"), also known as "Mele 'Ai Pōhaku" (the "Stone-Eating Song"), by Eleanor Kekoaohiwaikalani Wright Prendergast.

"Deepak Raga" is based on the mythological raga by Tansen, which when performed correctly makes fire, and is also inspired by the poem "To the Angelbeast" by Eduardo C. Corral.

"Malhar Raga" is another mythological raga by Tansen, which when performed correctly causes the rain to fall, and which must be performed with Deepak Raga, so as to prevent the earth from burning.

The quotation in the "Raimie" section of "My Name Is a Map" (*"Indian in color and British in taste . . ."*) is from Thomas Macaulay's "Minute on Indian Education."

"Orbit of Exterior Wildfires" uses the Kabirdas doha, probably written in the early 1500s by the poet-saint. A collection of dohe including this one appear at www.boloji.com.

ACKNOWLEDGMENTS

Grateful acknowledgement to the publications where some of these poems previously appeared.

Bamboo Ridge Journal: "Paper Lantern"
Crab Orchard Review: "Mynah"
EOAGH: "Indenture"
The Feminist Wire: "The River-Son's Betrayal," "Touch Me Not," and "Vivah at the Durga Temple"
Foundry Journal: "Malhar Raga"
Generations: "Emptying into the Sea" and "Fade"
Gulf Coast: "The Cowherd's Son"
Hawai'i Pacific Review: "Henna"
Hoppenthaler's Congeries (at *Connotation Press: An Online Artifact*): "Blind Man's Whist" and "Mantra"
Hyphen: "Diabetes Prayer" and "Tuberculosis"
Kartika Review: "Holi Lovesport"
The Margins (Asian American Writers' Workshop): "Back-Home Games in Florida" and "Dirge for Kamal"
The Ocean State Review: "Holi" and "Deepak Raga"
PANK: "Body of Myths"
Poem-a-Day (American Academy of Poets online): "Ode to Richmond Hill"
Soft Blow: "Bismillah" and "Standing on a Brampton Driveway Before the Threat of Snow"
Trikone Magazine: "South Queens Monsoon"

"Bound Coolie" and "Haunting" are included in the book *Writing Down the Walls: A Convergence of LGBTQ Voices* (edited by Helen Klonaris and Amir Rabiyah, Trans-Genre Press, 2015).

"Light the City" was included in the chapbook *na bad-eye me* (Pudding House Press, 2010), and "Cow Minah" in the chapbook *na mash me bone* (Finishing Line Press, 2011).

Thank you to the Kundiman community, including Cathy Linh Che, Sarah Gambito, Joseph Legaspi, Vikas Menon, and Oliver de la Paz.

Special thanks to Jeffrey Levine, Cassandra Cleghorn, Marie Gauthier, Jim Schley, and the team at Tupelo Press for believing in this work and selecting it for the Kundiman Prize.

Deepest gratitude to my teachers and mentors: Allison Adelle Hedge Coke, Nicole Cooley, Timothy Donnelly, Rigoberto González, Kimiko Hahn, Craig Santos Perez, Roger Sedarat, and Frank Stewart.

Thank you to the communities of The Home School, Oh, Bernice!, Queens College MFA program, the University of Hawai'i Department of English, and Voices of Our Nations Arts Foundation (VONA).

A special shukriya to friends and colleagues for their careful eyes, and for giving these poems homes, especially: Vidhu Aggarwal, Hari Alluri, Gaiutra Bahadur, Amalia Bueno, Karissa Chen, Faizal Deen, William Nu'utupu Giles, Kiala Givehand, Andil Gosine, Jaimie Gusman, Joseph Han, Gail Harada, John Hoppenthaler, Adhann Iwashita, Kima Jones, Lisa Linn Kanae, Akta Kaushal, Lee Kava, Charles Kell, Bryan Kuwada, Muriel Leung, Tyler McMahon, Michelle Meier, Elizabeth Onsuko, Jamaica Heolimeleikalani Osorio, Maura Pellettieri,

Trace Peterson, Tagi Qolouvaki, Noʻu Revillia, Anjoli Roy, Lyz Soto, Sarah Stetson, TC Tolbert, Aiko Yamashiro, and Emily Jungmin Yoon.

Thank you to my family for understanding.

And special thanks to Jordan Andrew Miles, always.

CPSIA information can be obtained
at www.ICGtesting.com
Printed in the USA
BVOW08s0249090118
504808BV00006B/11/P

9 781936 797967